LIFE OF THINE

...in the views of a versifier

BY
Tulasi

ISBN 978-93-5610-925-4

© Tulasi 2022

Published in India 2022 by Pencil

A brand of

One Point Six Technologies Pvt. Ltd.

123, Building J2, Shram Seva Premises,

Wadala Truck Terminal, Wadala (E)

Mumbai 400037, Maharashtra, INDIA

E connect@thepencilapp.com

W www.thepencilapp.com

Author biography

Born on 'World Poetry Day' (the 21st of March), Tulasi G is an M.Sc (I.T), B.Ed by qualification and a teacher by profession. She started her career as a Clerical Assistant at the State Bank of India and later decided to quit and pursue B.Ed as her calling was to become a teacher. She has worked as a Physics teacher and EVS co-ordinator at Innisfree House School, Bengaluru for 5 years. An alumnus of Carmel School (Padmanabhanagar), SKCH PU College, BMSCW, RVTC and University of Mysore, Tulasi had always been an ardent fan of literature and has taken part in many creative writing competitions and won prizes in them too. Though being a Science student and teacher now, she believes that a sound base in languages is very essential for comprehension of any subject.

She has guest authored an article titled 'Science Pedagogy in my classroom' for the website amicablescientists and has also won the consolation prize for her article 'Science in Superstition' in the IndianFolk article writing competition. She has also written a short story named 'Souvenir' and a poem named 'The Three Wise Monkeys'. Having 5 years of teaching experience, her students, both present and past, enjoy her classes not only for the way she teaches but mainly for being the adult who listens to them without judgement. Tulasi loves nature and philosophy and also believes that they both go hand in hand. She also believes that having a healthy mind is the first step towards having a healthy body.

Hence, she decided to write poems and stories that can motivate people, especially those who are anxious by nature.

Contents

Epigraph

"The strongest and heartfelt emotions are those that were left unsaid or have been unheard for long"

Foreword

I started writing poems in 2017. When I took breaks in between my work and studies, both happening simultaneously, I was left with very few options to pass time as going out and spending time would mean long gaps and the possibility of getting distracted from my main focus. That is when it struck me to put down on paper, whatever came to my mind about the different things around me and the experiences I had in daily life in the form of short poems. What started like a hobby gradually became a habit. Once the pandemic hit the world in 2020 and the lockdown brought face-to-face interactions to a halt of sorts, I observed that many people I knew started feeling anxious either due to fear of health issues or pay cuts or the future as a whole. That is when I realized that some of the poems that I wrote to self-motivate when I felt low could be published in the form of a book as words of positivity was the need of the hour. Hence, I have chosen 30 such pieces of work to make this collection.

Preface

In the current era, everyone we meet is stressed. Here is a collection of poems, which people can easily relate to, as everyone would want to hear some words of acknowledgement and motivation. The language of kindness can be understood by all. The poems here tell what one craves to hear when feeling low and what one should hear when feeling invincible. "Treat people the way you want to be treated and talk in a way you want to hear from someone else" is emphasized in these poems. The poems also talk of self-love, which is much needed for one's peace of mind. Teenagers and young adults go through a roller coaster of emotions in their lives and would want a channel that guides them in the right direction. These poems may be liked by any age group, however, will be of great use to the readers between 13 to 25 years of age. Being a teacher, and also in my personal experience, this is the fact I have realized.

~Tulasi

Acknowledgements

Thank God

Introduction

A poetic way of expressing what one wants to tell the world is both simple and complex at the same time. It is simple because poems don't include long descriptions of the poet's emotions unlike prose. It is complex because one needs to have some pattern or rhyme for the audience to connect better with a poem while in prose you just say what you need to say without following much of a format. The poems in this collection are free verse or freeform poetry though the poetess has used some rhyme to ease the flow of thoughts. There is no scheme or metre used here in these 30 poems.

13

Our Expectations in Life

A Conversation with God

Human Being:

I am your child dear Lord,
then why do you put me through trials?
Is it the consequence for some sort of a sin?
Life never goes as planned, by my accord
bearing the burden of problems, need to walk more miles;
what more do you want me to do to win?

God:

The light that keeps you going, like in the mid of cliffs, a fjord
my presence can only be felt and can't be bought in vials.
Tribulations are nothing to be considered chagrin
they are meant to make you strong, a bitter sweet reward.
Count your blessings, there are many I'm sure, they'll bring back
your smiles.
Know that I'm always with you, through both thick and thin.

Trustworthiness

A five letter word with a deep-set meaning,
it instils in a person, a very strong feeling.
When in someone you have faith, unshakeable and abundant,
what you get back is a lesson or a lifelong confidante.
"Be a reflection of what you wish to receive" is a common saying; my friend,
Loyalty and integrity are values that can never go out of trend.

If someone believes in you, learn to respect that;
instead of taking them for granted or brushing them under the mat.
Sure, one must be sincere and doubtless of people, and their words,
but have courage to leave those you trusted, if proved liars and cowards.
Trust is never old school as many consider,
too easy to break, years to build & revere.

APPRECIATION

A s you choose to do your best,

P eople around, often put you to test

P rogressing steadily, when you overcome each hurdle.

R egressive minds see you with a startle.

E fficiently do you execute your prowess?

C hanceless to render you, they will obsess.

I nvade the obstructions and reap all you sow,

A ny opportunity you see, grab it and grow.

T ime will tell them, there is none as good as you,

I nhibitions about self, though may bother a few…

O nly remember that, there's just one person you must trust;

N either Jack nor Jane, always applaud yourself first.

17

The Phases of Life
as we Grow

Spectrum of our Survival Span

Rising from a nine month sleep
as infants we learn to crawl and creep.

On our own feet, once we stand
from a toddler to a child our growth will expand.

Young and energetic, active too long
this phase of life we all wish could prolong…

Great is the time as an adolescent;
changes inside out without our consent.

Begin the responsibilities of a young adult;
youthdom's over, work for a living, now that's the cult.

Indications of wrinkles and grey hair
middle age crops in silently, now, that's not fair.

Values of the lifetime are the assets in dotage
this is the rainbow of life, the start of each stanza,
denoting every stage.

Veni Vidi Vici

Every person who saw you would be happy,
you will be crying so loud uncontrollably.
Even your parents would be happy seeing you;
that is the day you were born probably.

Phase 1: 'I came'

Growing up, you notice everything around,
pleasant or not, some even annoying to the core.
"You are too young. We know better" is what you hear often.
"Is my opinion not even worth considering?"
you would want to roar.

Phase 2: 'I saw'

After all those years of wait, you can finally take charge.
With responsibilities you also get your right.
Know right from wrong and choose the correct way.
Follow the path of helpfulness and raise your voice
for the needy, be it day or night.

Phase 3: 'I conquered'

Be Your Own Kind
of Beautiful

Have a Passion for Compassion

Kindness is a generous act which is innate.
Needy people would want our empathy, be considerate.
Let our actions speak and resonate.

Benevolence has no language, needs no translation,
for the giver it may mean nothing, but for the taker it
causes such elation.
Even animals perceive it without any cognition.

Care and understanding are rhapsody.
Those who show these are becoming scarce, a jeopardy...
Start today, you don't need to be Teresa's parody.

A simple act of kindness could go a long way.
Saint Nicolas showed it to children as he moved in his sleigh.
It is capable of putting an end to a fray.

Tenderness is a way of life not a separate quality.
Our warmth needs to be felt by all, that's equality.
Experience the power of amiability.

Be Your Own Kind of Beautiful

Every person cannot be a team player,
some need to be left alone.
Only then can they showcase their talent
Human beings have a unique zone.

Discrimination based on physical aspects
seems to be at a rise.
Do you want me to list out your shortcomings?
I think this threat is suffice.

The mind can play such cruel games on the victim,
you bullies may not know how it feels.
"It was just a casual joke." you may remark.
Understand, depression hardly reveals.

Some people even try to fit in the jigsaw
to avoid being isolated.
Doing so makes them a bully or they lose their identity;
unconsciously, their goodness is violated.

Now to the body shamed or bullied friends;
ignore those who comment,
they are no one to validate, you don't need to negotiate
to those who aren't relevant.

Focus on your life, you don't really know your worth.
Only to your conscience, you must be truthful.
Never hurt others for selfish reasons, but put them in
place if they act over smart;
and "Be Your Own Kind Of Beautiful!"

23

Assets from Childhood

The Joy of Little Things

Seeing a flower bloom in a plant you had sown
Brings immense pleasure for nothing.
Looking great in a simple dress when worn
Makes one fell happier than anything.

Neither a pot of gold nor winning a lottery
Can give one the joy of rain, on a sunny day;
What more can one ask for, like from memory's armoury
Than suddenly remembering the lyrics of a tune that you kept
trying to recall the other day?

Unexpectedly chancing upon a celebrity in a shop
you ask for a selfie or autograph, and they agree!
It feels like you are in seventh heaven atop
that emotion can't be expressed, the bliss of the highest degree!

Getting to have as breakfast, a dish you thought of asking last
night but forgot…
Now, that's gaiety
as though the universe conspired to help you achieve it,
quite a lot
thank the opportunity.

"The teacher is on leave" are words of euphoria
Especially if you aren't prepared for the class debate or viva
The class monitor who brought the news seems like Queen
Victoria
Rapturous is the least to say, as most in class, hail the diva.

Nostalgia

As I walk down the memory lane,
with nothing to lose nor a thing to gain,
my mind goes light and totally plain…

Reminiscences of the days that have passed
mumble within me as I see those photos amassed.
Bygone ages, those albums encompassed.

School benches, roadside shops or excursion dormitory,
each of them hold in them an indelible story.
Some are melancholic, while others, hunky dory!

Lapsed times are good to visit once a while
'cause they remind me of the lessons learnt, agile…
and also let me see how strong I grew from fragile.

They cross my mind making it go squiffy
that age when I loved Dexter and Miffy
Powerpuff girls and Popeye taught moral values in a jiffy.

Recollecting the 'g'olden era, of the life spent
is perfect as long as I don't forget the present;
since evocations must only be guides to LIVE this MOMENT!

Miracles

Eyelids drag close as you fall asleep in the living room
you hear your mom and dad calling you to the sleeping chamber
Too tired you choose to ignore and doze off in a slumber
However, the next morning, thanks to your parents, you wake up
in the boudoir.

"Ouch! My tooth fell off" you cried in pain.
"Don't worry" said your teacher "Place it below your pillow!"
As you look puzzled she continues "The tooth fairy will replace
it in your mouth again."
In a week's time it surely grows, whiter and harder than a
marshmallow.

Socks tied up in a winter month night,
hoping uncle Santa would fill them with Xmas gifts.
Next morrow as you see in daylight
Wishes granted as presents by adults at home, playing St. Nick's
role in night shifts.

Such simple things were held up in great esteem.
Your little minds had faith in considering these as pinnacles.
You age, realise the reasons for those as facts redeem.
Seeing is no more believing, but cherishing them till date as
miracles.

27

"Adolescents and Adults, be Role Models to Children "

A Child is *not* the Father
of the Man

A child while growing into adulthood exhibits some
natural traits,

more often than not;

but those are pretty fundamental,

not as vital as we thought.

What defines an adult is the competitiveness and rivalry,

that is a sign of selfishness.

Kids don't process search vengeance within;

they're innocent and filled with tenderness.

As one matures physically with feuds fought in mind,

it is obvious that they change.

Young minds have a wide spectrum before they face this world,

narrowing their trust's range.

Children inherit not just wealth but also character.

Parents, now the ball is in your court.

You don't need to sit and teach, they learn what they see.

Let them cultivate good values not just habits, ensure that

you are there to support.

The Magic Words

"Hello" with a smile, is a greeting, always gentle.
It refreshes the mood of the one who says and hears, that's its mettle.

"Excuse me" when requested, it is a way of justifying a fault politely,
the one who needs exempt you would also do it lightly.

"Please" you must say to show courtesy...
that will make the listener feel valued and a sense of ecstasy!

"Sorry" when you say, you don't lose anything.
Instead, the receiver will understand that your relationship matters to you more than everything.

"Thank You", these words exhibit your manners.
Gratitude is an important value one must imbibe with no planners.

"Welcome" is a reply to the one said above,
a polite response too is necessary now.

"Bye" when you say before you leave, makes the other person feel special;
looking forward for another meeting, they wave back, like you in their life are essential.

When Life Gives You Lemons, Make Lemonade

Greet the Changes

Metamorphoses in our anatomy
are the first signs of changes we see.
Changes happen every moment,
even time is not spared to be free...

Positive shifts are always welcome
wholeheartedly embrace them as they come.
Progress is what anyone would ask for,
for which transitions are to be accepted as they are, without any
war.

Negatives too come along the way
Optimism should then be held up and pessimism kept at bay.
Evolutions can only happen when you see both trough and crest
they too are means to grow to your best!

Move On, 'Coz, The Show Must Go On

If you are hurt by someone, let them go
If you are irritated by something, let it be
If you are attracted to negative folks, set them free.

When you feel aloof, it is just a thought, let it go
When you feel angry, it is momentary, let it be
When you find yourself overthinking, set yourself free.

If others cry because of you, say sorry, let it go
If others shout at you, they are stressed, let it be
If others seem to be too dominating, set them free.

When life gives you lemons, let it go
When life goes out of track, let it be
When life looks empty, set it free.

You make life beautiful, not anyone, let them go
You must feel happy no matter what, let it be
You are in charge of your life, nothing else, set them free.

Life is like a Train Journey

Life is like a train journey
can be curvy, and at times, smooth like a symphony.
Nothing is permanent along this path,
you look back, what you see is a different path.

We see all new faces, as we board the rail
some smiling, some serious, and a few sleepy and frail.
There may be a few who start a conversation
though they know it won't last till the destination.

Not all who started with you come all the way, don't beseech
and you too may get off before others, train journeys teach.
Life is nothing different, here too you meet many people
Avoid attachments, don't take everyone seriously, except those
that set an example.

Only a few near your seat
would converse with you or greet
that's essential; in case of emergencies that occur undue
it will be these people that come to your rescue.

Welcomes and Goodbyes

Beginnings are the toughest.
Irrespective of who you are
changes always make you skip a heartbeat.
That's how it has been so far.

Welcomes are exciting however
as change is the only constant.
Be open to it, that'll reduce the worry.
Enjoy what is there with you, this instant.

Events start when another ends
those can make us halt.
Nature works that way usually
don't blame, not anyone's fault.

Goodbyes can be bittersweet
but leave a lot of memories.
Reminisce them and cherish them
at a later date, they are what remain our life's stories.

35

Adapting to the World;
Without Losing Track

'Smart' Phones

'Smart'phones: do they really match their name's meaning?
Of course they do, but their owner, the antonym.
They are easy to carry around
as they fit into any purse or pockets of one's Denim.

Radios and transistors were once the only sources of music.
Compact than gramophones, they served their true purpose.
Smartphones have replaced them all too, rendering them useless
not only audio, wherever you are, even videos can be viewed
during recess.

Television was a craze in the 80s and 90s.
Though called an idiot box, making one a couch potato,
they united the family to watch favourite shows.
Now people watch everything in phones, sometimes incognito.

Computers were only seen in cyber cafes.
Internet was only for officials.
Smartphones have taken over from them too.
Use of technology is what we are doing unknowingly, we
millennials.

Mr. Graham Bell invented phones as a mode to communicate.
These, do that the least, though they borrow the name.
With so many apps and messengers available in Playstores
for free
calling people is a rare effort one takes after these came.

Heritage vs Culture

When customs are inherited they become heritage.
Ancestors formulated them according to that age.
They are meant to enrich our values and morals
and also bring to our country its laurels.

What we create now based on our present lifestyle,
that doesn't interfere with societal norms and profile,
culture is its name, something common to a majority.
It can be diverse as there are many people, some gain popularity.

These two are terms that are generally mixed.
Synonyms they aren't, neither are they fixed.
Heritage to an extent may be, but culture's variable.
The only common factor is that they have made us gullible.

Credulous people follow them as superstition
Millennials try to reason out scientifically, every tradition.
Those of you who due to half knowledge or influence, defy,
they are meant to civilize the citizens and get them to unify.

Homosapiens - Today's World, in an Early human's Point of View

I hunted only when I was hungry
or when I was in danger by an animal.
We had harmony generally in our times
not like jealous humans now; fights for selfish
reasons where minimal.

We did not think of the future or brood over the past
just ate fresh fruits or grilled meat.
We settled down later for agriculture
not to snatch lands from the jungle, just wanted at the
end of the day, a simple home to retreat.

Fire discovered and wheels invented;
both for a purpose each.
One to cook and keep us warm, the other to move
things quickly.
Today you have a list of discoveries and inventions,
far from my intellect's reach.

Everything, when utilised efficiently
are boons to human kind"
But what are you doing with all that you have?"
Aimlessly squandering, "Have you lost your mind?"

If you choose to continue these ways
you'll soon plunder the Earth and each of its resource
and probably return to our times.
Wake up before it's too late to be left with only remorse.

Knowing Thyself

Who's Your True Friend?

A friend in need is a friend indeed;
following whose guidance, a better life you can lead.
You don't have to explain to them nor do you have to plead.
Ideal friendships are shown in films and books on them,
good to read.

Casual acquaintances are called friends too.
They nod in favour to whatever you do.
Real friends are those who speak to your face
without giving any clue.
Those gems are pretty hard to find, honest people are so few.

Sieving powder is easier, unlike people, it works.
You won't be able to distinguish genuine ones from jerks.
Now that's a pity! But let that thought sink in even if it irks.
However, interactions do make you wise, those are the perks.

The best kind of counsellor is someone else you don't realise.
Only this person knows cent percent about you from birth to
your demise.
Not that childhood friend of yours, relatives not even close,
not even your parents recognise.
To finalize, let me tell that only YOU are your true friend,
much to many people's surprise.

SIGNATURE

S ymbolises who you are
hows that you have worked to come so far.

I dentity it is, make it so powerful
t must show your value, the pen when you pull.

G ive a font so tough to forge
et it so unique, let few letters merge.

N ot just that, it must leave a lasting impact
ever should it be so confusing, keep it legible and intact.

A nyone who sees it must appreciate
utograph it can become, noble deeds when you initiate.

T his when put on a book is of no much use
he same thing when put on a document can transduce.

U nder no circumstance should you forget how you sign
nmatched if it seems, you may sit and whine.

R emember to thank your teachers, not casting a thumb
impression shows you are a literate
aise your voice and sign when you need to help those who can't,
be considerate.

E veryone at first, must be an amateur
nsure that your dream becomes your signature.

Serenity - Enjoying the Calm of 'Being Quiet'

Power of Tranquility

A weekday afternoon, on a calm beach side,
on a highway road with no traffic when you ride,
in even a forest camp, between the Woods, when you reside,
that's when, the peace within, you choose to confide.

Situations tend to ebb and flow like a tide,
you can't control it nor from it can you hide.
Instead learn to take it all with the stride.
Like an eagle, soar above it and glide.

It all depends on how one is from inside
which is an individual's choice to decide.
Serenity comes upon us when we abide
by our mind and not the heart we need to take as guide.

The quieter you are, the listening span becomes wide.
Commotions in and out need to be pushed aside.
Focus and observe without letting the attention divide.
Ataraxia can be achieved one day when you do,
which will be your pride.

Silence is Golden

Buddha preferred to be calm.
He said don't be angry with another,
that will only harm your peace of mind.
Instead, ignore their presence, you'll feel as light as a feather.

"How do I achieve this?" one may ask.
That's simple, learn to silence your mind.
He practiced doing so even amidst chaos;
that may not be simple, he was one of his kind.

"Can I become Buddha?" now that's a tough question."
One must be, not become" according to me
Enlightenment can come to you, anywhere, anytime.
It is all in the mind, not the place, you see.

Silence is Golden, unnecessary words are meaningless.
The ignorance of this, is definitely not a bliss.
Break your silence only when your words have more value.
This is a principle one must follow, "Don't miss!"

45

Qualities to Acquire

'日本' Japan, The Land of The RISING

A country that stands as a role model.
No calamities, both natural and otherwise, can make it toddle.
The citizens' grit and will power act as a paddle.

Wabi Sabi, is accepting transience and imperfection.
Make the world bow to them in veneration.
Pat your back Jack, now and in future generation.

Kintsugi, glorifies and celebrates the flaws.
This art of gold, truly needs an applause.
Mistakes are precious lessons, it tells us for a cause.

Kensho, reminds one to be a true reflection of self.
No pretence in fear of judgements, a value in itself.
Pushing aside all prejudices, one learns to accept oneself.

Kaizen - the philosophy of improvement for the better.
It has the world class message to be a trend setter.
We need to inculcate it in our lives, to every letter.

Savvy thy Ikigai or the purpose of this life on Earth.
and everything we practise must shout out its worth.
There is no dearth of people in the globe, make yours a
noble birth.

'Devotion', Pure Love

Certain things in life are basic.
This is called as need
Irrespective of who you are and what you do
Necessities don't recede.
With these comes OBLIGATION.

Up next come those cravings that are tempting.
There is no urgency to have them, but still we would want.
Desires are what we have to show off.
They aren't even useful sometimes, but still we flaunt.
With these comes POSSESSION.

Now you have the money to buy some stuff.
We term this as demand.
No one has to get this for us.
"I have paid, so I must have it as I wish" I can command.
With these comes STIPULATION.

The worst emotion comes up when you are dissatisfied.
Well, no person can satisfy greed.
Jealousy and envy too accompany this…
Once trapped by this, the person can't be freed.
With these comes OBSESSION.

One is able to overcome all these and see.
Here comes the greatest form of love.
The ultimate form of selflessness and trust…
A fine feeling that has nothing above.
With these comes DEVOTION!

Taking a Chill Pill

Realms of Fantasy

As I retire to bed in hope of good dreams,
my eyelids come together, yet something gleams;
a flow of thoughts unconsciously streams.

Marvellous places and wonderful people I greet.
I wonder how till date we didn't meet!
Everything happening appears to be so sweet.

Sometimes, all of a sudden, someone seems to chase.
Nightmares are dreams too that by morning have no trace.
I never want to see those again, dear mind, please erase.

Dr. APJ Abdul Kalam said, "Dreams don't let you sleep!"
Such a visionary he was, its meaning is so deep...
Work smart to achieve them, 'coz what you sow, you reap.

At times a lash falls on the cheeks, askew.
I place it on the back of my palm, make a wish before
away it blew.
Who knows sometimes, dreams do come true!

Hakuna Matata

Past can't be revisited.
Future can't be forecasted.
Live the moment which is in your hand.
Hakuna Matata!

You can't change the world.
Be the change you want unfurled.
That would probably set an example.
Hakuna Matata!

Curiosity kills the cat and makes one anxious.
Depression about past event? Why so serious?
Relax, let it all go.
Hakuna Matata!

What others think or how they behave,
is a reflection of their lifestyle, let it engrave
Irrespective of what they are, you spread the Upendi.
Hakuna Matata!

51

We Grow Through What We Go Through

Phoenix, the Saga of Women

Every day, coming home safe is like a civil war conquered,
there's no argumentation.
Stop this bullying right now, no more procrastination.
There's at least one case of assault reported each week.
What's happening to us fellow citizens? Can't we speak up?
Are we so meek?

Let's teach all children we know, irrespective of their gender,
that harassment and abuse are 'anti-social services' to tender.
Candle marches, after an incident, don't serve the purpose.
Of course, it's a protest, but be the main singer to be heard,
not just sing in chorus.

Not only strangers, betrayals come from those familiar friends
who turned foe.
We are living human beings, not articles that you use and throw.
Put yourself in our shoes, it may be tough to empathise, but
possible.
Remember that each one who asks from the society must also
be responsible.

Any wronged lady is a daughter, a sister or a mother of someone.
Now the onus is on you, dear men, to be her father, brother or
son.
Springing up from the ashes of all these daily disgrace…
Like a phoenix, women emerge with a smile, hiding all their
fears & still in a daze.

Cries of the Neglected Gender

"Be a man.", "Boys don't cry." These are the commonly
heard phrases.
They have feelings too and would want to pour out in
certain cases.
If you see a vulnerable man, don't judge him without any bases.

Not all men are alike; "Men will be men" is a myth.
Have you seen them all, to generalise or compare with?
Blame game and stereotyping masculinity has reached the zenith.

Freedom of expression to women is always welcome.
Feminism was meant to overcome bias, not what it now has
become.
Few among us seem to be misusing this word, an unexpected
outcome.

Birth as a male is their destiny.
Those misinterpreting feminism are fuelling men's agony.
Can exhibiting misandry solve misogyny?

I thank those gentlemen and their patience I revere
No false accusations to avenge for some other mutual issues,
that's severe
I sincerely apologise to men, on behalf of those, due to whom,
you may today, have no career.

A gentle reminder female folks, there are many good men out
there.
Pushing them all beyond a limit will make their existence rare.
Please understand that most men don't know to express,
but they really do CARE.

Notes

Write Your Thoughts Below

54